Michael Bungay Stanier

GREAT

short, sharp shots of inspiration

WORK

served up daily

PROVOCATIONS

Great Work Provocations
Short, sharp shots of inspiration

By Michael Bungay Stanier

Box of Crayons Press

Published by Box of Crayons Press, Toronto, Ontario, Canada.

First edition printed 2013 in the United States.

For permission requests, write to the publisher at admin@boxofcrayons.biz

Box of Crayons Press
137 Marion St
Toronto, ON M6R 1E6
Canada

Cover and text designed by Ana Garza-Robillard.

ISBN: 978-0-9784407-3-2

Quantity discounts are available on bulk purchases of this book. Special books or book excerpts can also be created to fit specific needs. For information, please email Michael@BoxofCrayons.biz.

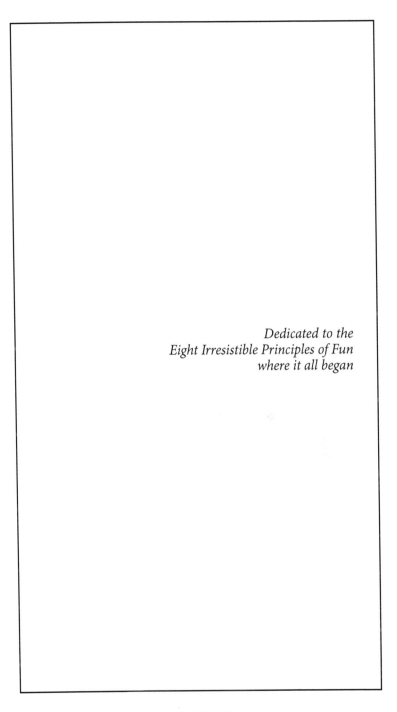

Dedicated to the
Eight Irresistible Principles of Fun
where it all began

Want more from your work?

There are only three types of work in your life.

There's **Bad Work:** the mind-numbing, soul-sapping, life-crushing work that grows like weeds. In organizations it's bureaucracy, pointless meetings, email overwhelm … and anything that makes you think, "This is my one and precious life - what am I doing?"

Then there's **Good Work:** your job description, and what you spend most of your time doing.

And finally there's **Great Work:** the meaningful work you're hungry for.

This is the work that matters, makes a difference and has an impact. It's the work you actually want to tell people about. (Who boasts, "I didn't get too far behind on my email today!"?)

If you're like most of us, you are struggling just to stay on top of the regular stuff that keeps flowing your way. Like digging a hole in the sand at the beach, no matter how fast you bail, it keeps filling up with water.

Bottom line? You want to do more Great Work but you're struggling to get beyond the Bad and the Good. In my book *Do More Great Work* I offer a systematic way you can find, start and sustain your Great Work.

This book is different.

Great Work Provocations was designed to wake you up, provoke you and shake you out of the Good Work rut on a daily basis.

It draws from my background in the worlds of change, creativity and innovation, and from my love of a good metaphor and a powerful question.

If you've ever wanted to get beyond the day-to-day and do more Great Work, this book is for you.

Yours,

PS - you can get your free Great Work Provocation as a daily email from www.BoxofCrayons.biz/provoked

If Mt Everest were a building, it would be

2,472

stories high.

What's the peak you're aiming at?

What if you boldly lifted your sights even higher?

FOCUS.

And then refocus.

And then refocus.

Stomp distractions today.

MICHAEL BUNGAY STANIER

At whom are you pointing the finger?

What if, instead, you took responsibility?

What shifts?

Rope.

Compass.

Map.

Matches.

What would serve you best today?

MICHAEL BUNGAY STANIER

Persistence is an extraordinarily powerful strategy. Just look at the Grand Canyon.

What's worth trying for again?

It's easy to be a cynic. It's wonderful to be delighted.

MICHAEL BUNGAY STANIER

Momentum is only useful when you're heading in the right direction.

Let's assume you're moving.

Are you going where you want to go?

JANUARY
7

ZOOS MAKE LOTS OF MONEY FROM SELLING THE MANURE OF THEIR ANIMALS.

WHAT ARE YOU CURRENTLY DISCARDING THAT MIGHT BE OF VALUE TO SOMEONE ELSE?

MICHAEL BUNGAY STANIER

Are you noticing the waves or the deeper currents?

Are you a C or a D?

(Create & Collaborate Dominate & Delegate)

Be honest now.

MICHAEL BUNGAY STANIER

Stop talking about it. Draw it. Now look at the picture and then do it.

Is it time to turn it up?

Is it time to turn it off?

MICHAEL BUNGAY STANIER

I was going to write something about procrastination today ... but I'm going to do that tomorrow instead.

Wisdom enters through the wound.

Is it time to hurt a little?

Go say hello to someone you don't yet know.

HELLO
my name is

MICHAEL BUNGAY STANIER

Do you understand the rules well enough to rebel?

MICHAEL BUNGAY STANIER

The Critical Few.

The Trivial Many.

Where's your focus?

JANUARY
17

Time to scatter seeds?

Or prune the growth?

MICHAEL BUNGAY STANIER

Try out a new space to work in.

See what the shift in perspective brings.

**JANUARY
19**

What's the tempting thing to do today?

MICHAEL BUNGAY STANIER

Write down what's making you anxious.

Seeing it straight often makes it shrink and lose power.

JANUARY
21

TODAY, SHOULD YOU GIVE OR SHOULD YOU TAKE?

MICHAEL BUNGAY STANIER

Aethelred
the Unready.
Conan the Crooked.
Charles the Lame.
All great kingly
names from
times past.

What might your title
be? What would you
like it to be?

(I always wanted to
be Michael
the Surprised.)

"Employee engagement" sounds like something someone does to you.

But really, you need to do it yourself.

MICHAEL BUNGAY STANIER

Who are you protecting? Is it time to let them face the music by themselves?

JANUARY
25

What can you simplify?

MICHAEL BUNGAY STANIER

What are you tolerating?

Is it tolerable people, work, recognition, behavior, or something else?

Think back
five years.
Impossible to
have foreseen
where you are
now and what's
going on, isn't it?

I hope you're not
taking your plans
too seriously....

Is this the moment when you upgrade the conversation from email to a phone call?|

MICHAEL BUNGAY STANIER

Today, make Freedom your guide.

MICHAEL BUNGAY STANIER

You can offer up "the hard truth" in a way that creates growth or that shuts it down.

What's the hard truth you need to hear right now?

Delegate, delegate, delegate.

MICHAEL BUNGAY STANIER

What are you assuming about their intentions?

Do you have any data for that, or have you made it all up?

FEBRUARY
2

Are you showing up for a job description?

Or are you showing up for a cause?

MICHAEL BUNGAY STANIER

Are you monologuing?

When did you stop listening?

FEBRUARY

4

WHERE ARE YOU THE BOTTLENECK?

HOW WILL YOU UNBLOCK THE FLOW?

MICHAEL BUNGAY STANIER

Ever feel shackled by your own schedule?

How might you pick the locks today?

Stop something.

Start something.

Do more of something.

Pick one.

MICHAEL BUNGAY STANIER

Sometimes it's the quick and the dead. And sometimes the quick are the dead. Slow down a bit today.

What if the way things are right now is perfect?

MICHAEL BUNGAY STANIER

Delete 20 emails that you know are just using up space in your inbox.

Don't read them in detail or reply. Just delete.

Look before you leap. He who hesitates is lost.

Which would serve you best today?

90% of people consider themselves above average drivers.

Where might you be glossing over your actual ability?

What might you do to strengthen it?

MICHAEL BUNGAY STANIER

More selfish. More self-less.

Which would be most powerful today?

MICHAEL BUNGAY STANIER

Some part of you is rusting up.

Which part? And how can you provide some lubrication?

Break rules.

Stick to principles.

MICHAEL BUNGAY STANIER

Keep your promises.

(Even the little ones.)

FEBRUARY
16

Where are
you standing
on that
spectrum that
runs from
self-interest
to service?

MICHAEL BUNGAY STANIER

Blow on the embers?

Or dowse the flame?

How could you change the intensity?

FEBRUARY
18

Exhale.

MICHAEL BUNGAY STANIER

The paradox is that creativity needs boundaries to flourish.

How could you tighten the parameters?

Get out of the office.

Get into the field.

What's your "field"? (It's where the people you serve spend time.)

MICHAEL BUNGAY STANIER

What's your idea of freedom?

If you took full responsibility for getting there, what would change?

FEBRUARY
22

What if that report had to be a page, or a paragraph, or a picture, or the 140 characters of a Tweet?

Keep stripping things down.

MICHAEL BUNGAY STANIER

You'll worry a lot less about what people think of you when you realize how little time anyone spends thinking about you.

They're too busy with their own stuff.

FEBRUARY
24

Is it time to push a little harder?

Or is it time to take it a little easier?

And what does that look like for you?

What's a boomerang that doesn't come back?

A stick.

What can you get off your plate?

What's useful to throw away today?

In 10 years time, you won't remember what you're worrying about now.

Knowing that - can you put it aside?

MICHAEL BUNGAY STANIER

Today, give something your total, undivided, rigorous, tunnel-vision focus.

No distractions. No surfacing for air.

FEBRUARY 28/29

Slow train.

Fast car.

Long flight.

Which choice would serve you best today?

MICHAEL BUNGAY STANIER

A small team might just be the most powerful force for change within a company: small enough to be flexible and strong enough to be resilient.

MARCH
2

What's working?

How can you amplify that?

MICHAEL BUNGAY STANIER

Comfortable is just boredom with good P.R.

How can you stir things up?

MARCH
4

If you want
to think
differently,

move.

Sitting at the
same desk in
the same way =
the same
thoughts.

MICHAEL BUNGAY STANIER

If you had to pick a role model from those around you, who would it be?

What are they doing that's catching your eye?

On a scale of 1 to 7, how much will you care about the experience of those you interact with today?

And what does that look like?

MICHAEL BUNGAY STANIER

Stick up your hand and say, "It's my fault."

Once that's out of the way, you can get on with finding the solution.

Finish any gathering by asking: What will you do and by when?

Just so you know that they know, that you know that they know what needs to be done.

MARCH
9

MICHAEL BUNGAY STANIER

If you're part of a team, you'll be sharing a common goal.

Do you think everyone has exactly the same destination in mind?

Invite the skeptics in. They're desperate to be proven wrong.

But avoid the cynics. They've already made their minds up.

Today, make **COURAGE** your guide.

MICHAEL BUNGAY STANIER

Apply this insight to something you're doing right now:

Madness is doing the same thing over and over again, expecting a different result.

MICHAEL BUNGAY STANIER

Orchestra.
Baseball team.
Beehive.
Commandos.

What's the best metaphor for your team?

What are the pros and cons?

Think about 12 months from now.

What do you want to boast about then that you could start doing today?

MARCH
15

MICHAEL BUNGAY STANIER

Focus is one of the bonds that keeps the team together.

Where are you leaking focus?

MARCH
16

Tidy up. Make a mess.

Either way, change normal.

MICHAEL BUNGAY STANIER

Have the conversation you've been putting off.

MARCH
18

Pressure builds diamonds.

Grit creates pearls.

What's the disruption that's allowing your creativity to thrive?

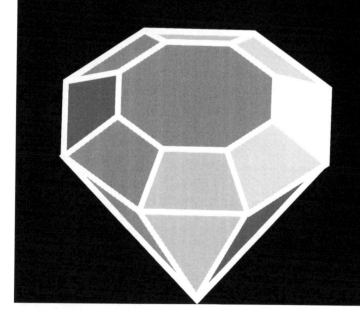

The way power works is often unspoken and invisible.

Put on your x-ray vision glasses. Where are the power lines?

Generously and whole-heartedly give someone full credit today.

What an awesome gift - for them and for you.

MICHAEL BUNGAY STANIER

Working out =
exercise hard
and rest.

Working =
long, slow
grind.

**Only one of
those builds
muscle.**

Flash flood vs. drip irrigation.

One's spectacular and the other lets the crops grow.

What's your style?

MARCH
23

MICHAEL BUNGAY STANIER

What if courage today meant just a small step rather than a big leap.

What would the small step be?

MARCH 24

Which one's winning out in your life: Me? Or We?

And how's that working out for you?

MARCH
25

MICHAEL BUNGAY STANIER

If no one is pushing back, then you're not even close to the edge.

MICHAEL BUNGAY STANIER

Odds are you're chronically tired.

What chance of getting to bed early tonight to catch up a little?

MICHAEL BUNGAY STANIER

Whatever you're working on, make it a crappy first draft.

(EVERY first draft sucks. EVERY first draft is vital in getting this thing on the road.)

We are always testing a hypothesis.

What's yours, and what's the evidence you're gathering?

MICHAEL BUNGAY STANIER

Fully commit to something.

MARCH
30

The bigger,
the better.

The best
things come
in small
packages.

**Which would
serve you
best today?**

MARCH
31

MICHAEL BUNGAY STANIER

Zoom out. What's the big picture?

Now zoom in. With this new information, what's the immediate need?

APRIL

1

Who deserves a trophy?

How could you give them one?

Stop something.
Start something.
Do more of something.

APRIL
3

Break the process you're working on down into the smallest of steps.

Now start eliminating, adding and amplifying them.

Make the process really work.

MICHAEL BUNGAY STANIER

That thing you're putting off? How about you knock it off the list right now.

Set aside the time you need … and just do it.

If you had to "blank slate it" and start again, how would you rebuild your job description?

MICHAEL BUNGAY STANIER

Don't rehearse.

That just sets you up to get lost when things depart from your script.

But prepare.

What you can't control, you can't control - so no point in worrying.

What you can control you will control - so no point in worrying.

Make the first answer a YES today.

What are you assuming about their intentions?

Do you have any data for that, or have you made it all up?

MICHAEL BUNGAY STANIER

Is it time to surface and look at the big picture?

Or time to get gritty with the details?

APRIL
11

You're at a crossroads.

What's the decision you need to make?

Which road will you turn down?

MICHAEL BUNGAY STANIER

"Tension is who you think you should be. Relaxation is who you are."
- Chinese proverb

Are you tense or relaxed? What's the wisdom here?

Make a list of the top 3 things you're currently tolerating. Grim reading, isn't it?

Why not shift one of those things today.

MICHAEL BUNGAY STANIER

Chisel.
Shredder.
Glue gun.

Which tool would serve you best today?

APRIL
15

Strategy is a visual art. Draw what matters.

CREATE A MAP.

Are you advancing or retreating?

APRIL

17

This is the simplest model of them all.

Is it a Yes? Is it a No?

Which one is it?

MICHAEL BUNGAY STANIER

On a scale of 1 to 7, how much fun will you create today?

And what will that look like?

Who might be most surprised - and most grateful - today when you ask, "How can I help?"

MICHAEL BUNGAY STANIER

If only we knew what we knew.

How can you use the wisdom in the room?

APRIL
21

What if you stopped looking up and looking down and instead looked across, horizontally, for help?

What do you see there?

ARE YOU MAKING A PATH OR FOLLOWING A PATH?

What's the project you're longing for someone to give you?

How about you go ask for it? Or, bolder still, just take it.

MICHAEL BUNGAY STANIER

Today, make Generosity your guide.

What's the gift you're bringing to the people you work with today?

Be specific and clear about this.

MICHAEL BUNGAY STANIER

Inefficiency is an inevitable precursor to efficiency… except when it's just inefficiency.

Are you making progress or not?

What's the thing you should walk away from?

Loyalty has its limits.

MICHAEL BUNGAY STANIER

Today, what's the one thing you want?

APRIL
29

TRY THAT OUT AS THE STRUCTURE FOR YOUR NEXT PRESENTATION OR MEETING.

Less polishing.

More delivering.

Step out of
the centre
and over to
the edge.

What's the
view like
from there?

MAY
2

MICHAEL BUNGAY STANIER

Learning and growth come when you're in the 'consciously incompetent' state. Not fun but useful.

Time to shift off a comfortable plateau?

The way through to easy is nearly always through what's difficult.

MICHAEL BUNGAY STANIER

What are you learning from your boss? Not so much on the technical side of things, but on the "way things work (or don't work)" side of the equation?

Today you get an A+. Nice job.

Now, what has to happen for you to earn it?

At any moment, 60% of the planet is covered by clouds.

Where might you be hungering for sunshine and not seeing that the clouds are part of the journey?

MICHAEL BUNGAY STANIER

If you were playing the long game (and you are, whether you like it or not), what would you sacrifice now for the bigger win?

MICHAEL BUNGAY STANIER

MAY
8

Information's seductive when it's TBU: True But Useless.

Try hitting delete.

You pay a price in energy and impact when you multitask.

So do it responsibly. Maybe try just a little less, a little more often.

MICHAEL BUNGAY STANIER

Think of yesterday's high point.

What's the lesson there for you?

You control way less than you think, but you influence way more than you believe.

How about flexing your influence muscles today.

MICHAEL BUNGAY STANIER

WOMBAT

Not the fuzzy cute Australian mammal but this: Waste Of Money Bandwidth And Time.

What's your **WOMBAT**?

**MAY
13**

Take 15 minutes today and clear away some of the junk.

Wouldn't it be great if "they" got their act together? Of course, you're most likely someone's "they" as well.

Knowing this, what will you do differently?

Today, shine a light in a dark corner.

MAY
16

MICHAEL BUNGAY STANIER

On a scale
of 1 to 7, how
courageous
will you be
today? And
what does
that look
like?

Of course you've got goals.

But when did you last look at them? And are they really challenging and specific?

MAY
18

MICHAEL BUNGAY STANIER

Go deep?

Or go wide?

MAY
19

What are you attached to? And what's the price you're paying for that attachment?

(This message brought to you by the four noble truths of Buddhism.)

The people who got rich in the Gold Rush sold shovels.

What if you stopped digging and figured out how to provide digging tools today?

MICHAEL BUNGAY STANIER

What does your boss's boss think of all this?

Not sure?

Might be worth finding out.

MICHAEL BUNGAY STANIER

You start the day with good intentions, but somehow by lunchtime it's gone to pieces.

Just refocus and start again. It's not too late.

What's the routine that has you stuck?

MICHAEL BUNGAY STANIER

MAY
24

Today, how will you measure success?

(Just one thing.)

MAY
25

Given the
choice between
giving advice
and asking
a question,
ask a question.
Why?
A good question
opens up new
possibilities
and new neural
pathways.

MICHAEL BUNGAY STANIER

Somewhere, someone in your life needs a clearer No than you're currently giving them.

How about you do that today?

MAY
27

LOOK BACK, PICK SOMETHING AND CELEBRATE IT.

How are you
waiting to be
rescued?

Hoping for a
miracle?

Indulging in
magical thinking?

Instead,
ask yourself,
"What's the
reality here?

When you're working with someone, come to it with the attitude of "my friend's amazing."

And sure enough, they are.

MICHAEL BUNGAY STANIER

Be here now.
Plan for the next generation.

Which would serve you best today?

**MAY
31**

If you were
an athlete,
you'd be
striving
for your
"personal
best".
Yes, you're
an athlete.

MICHAEL BUNGAY STANIER

Wines get their unique taste from their terroir - the soil in which the vines grow.

From where are your roots drawing their nourishment?

And how is that showing up in you now?

Ulysses had to be tied to the mast to avoid the tempting songs of the Sirens who would otherwise lure his boat onto the rocks.

What or who are your Sirens?

What or who is your mast?

It's the wrong hole.

Please.
Stop.
Digging.

MICHAEL BUNGAY STANIER

What have you become addicted to?

Email?
Fear?
Meetings?
Rebellion?
Success?
Routine?
Your own
expectations?

MICHAEL BUNGAY STANIER

A statistic from the UK: power drills are used for an average of 20 minutes throughout their entire lifespan.

What are you holding on to "just in case" that it's now time to let go?

Before you go crazy about what's not working, take a moment to notice what is.

What are the top three things that are working well for you right now?

MICHAEL BUNGAY STANIER

You tried and it didn't work.

Did you give up? Or just figure out an alternative way forward?

(Either one of those might be the right answer.)

No doubt you started on this (whatever "this" is for you) for a good reason.

But just to check - is that reason still alive, good and valid?

MICHAEL BUNGAY STANIER

How do you get "hooked"?

What does it look like?

How do you behave?

Where's the wisdom in this for you?

JUNE
10

DON'T YOU LOVE IT WHEN YOU (METAPHORICALLY OR LITERALLY) CATCH ALL THE GREEN LIGHTS?

HOW COULD YOU GIVE SOMEONE ELSE THE GREEN LIGHT TODAY?

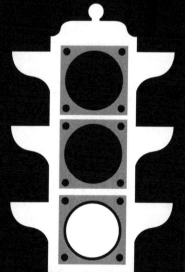

What's the easy thing to do?

What's the fun thing to do?

What would have the most impact?

So what will you do?

JUNE
12

On a scale of 1-10 (with 1 being low), how do you rate yourself as "victim" right now?

What choice do you need to make to nudge that number downward?

MICHAEL BUNGAY STANIER

Are you confusing doing what's hard with doing what's valuable?

JUNE
14

To what would you like to make a stronger, bolder commitment?

What's the strong **No** that would allow you to make that bold **Yes?**

MICHAEL BUNGAY STANIER

You understand your position.

But what if you truly "stepped into" the position of the person across the desk from you.

What do you notice from there?

JUNE
16

What's the one thing that would make the task easier today?

Who can you ask for help to find it?

Imagine this:
you and your
team raising
the pirate flag.

What are the
new rules?
And what
are you doing
differently
now?

Who's a source of inspiration for you?

When did you last check in with what they're up to?

MICHAEL BUNGAY STANIER

If there were a Society for the Prevention of Cruelty to People at Work, what would they come in and change at your place?

JUNE
20

Ask at the start of the next meeting, "What do we need to do to make this meeting awesomely useful rather than tediously predictable?"

OK, maybe not the second half of that.

JUNE
21

MICHAEL BUNGAY STANIER

Should you head to the jungle?

Or cultivate the garden?

GREAT WORK PROVOCATIONS

Magic can happen when you bring together two unexpected things and blend them or bind them.

What's something unexpected you might throw into the mix?

MICHAEL BUNGAY STANIER

Stuff - stuff you do, stuff you have - expands to fill the time and the space you give it.

Keep trimming the bottom 10%.

JUNE
24

A FAKE SMILE:
just the teeth.

A GENUINE SMILE:
the little eye
muscles also
crinkle up.

People can instinctively
tell the difference.
Keep an eye out today
for the real connection.

MICHAEL BUNGAY STANIER

One of the deep paradoxes of life: it all matters and none of it really matters.

What I find in that is another paradox: both commitment and freedom.

If this were a story, who'd be the hero? Who'd be the villain? What if the roles were reversed?

What do you see now from this new perspective?

MICHAEL BUNGAY STANIER

If the level of commitment you were displaying now were, say, 7/10 - what would full commitment look like?

What would be different?

Let's just say
your Plan A
isn't working.
(At least, not as
well as it might.)
What's Plan
B? And what if
you start some
things moving
on that right
now?

JUNE
29

MICHAEL BUNGAY STANIER

If you ask a question, wait and listen to the answer.

That listening part happens less often than you might think.

What's the crossroad you're currently facing?

What are the alternatives from which you need to choose?

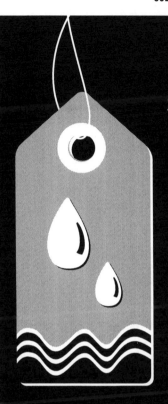

Water is a strange and miraculous liquid. It's the only molecule whose solid state - ice - is lighter than its liquid state.

It's one of the key reasons why life can flourish on Earth.

Today, what can you float above rather than let it drag you down?

MICHAEL BUNGAY STANIER

What if you got tired of tolerating that thing and did something about it?

MICHAEL BUNGAY STANIER

What deserves your passionate and intense focus today?

JULY
4

40% of what we do is habit or in other words, unconscious.

Where do you need to wake up?

MICHAEL BUNGAY STANIER

Rather than focus on the behaviour you want to change, start noticing the trigger that sets off that behaviour. When X happens, I do Y.

What's your Y? What's its X?

Just enjoy all the good stuff.

MICHAEL BUNGAY STANIER

You can sprint and rest, sprint and rest. Or you can run long and slow.

But you can't keep sprinting.

So what needs to change?

JULY
8

IN CYCLING JARGON
KOM STANDS FOR
"KING OF THE
MOUNTAIN"
- THE CYCLIST WHO WINS
THE RACE TO THE TOP OF
THE PEAK.

WHAT'S THE PEAK YOU'RE
HEADING FOR? WHAT
WILL IT TAKE TO GET
ACROSS THE LINE FIRST?

Is it time to polish? Or do you need to keep sanding it down?

JULY
10

What's happening in the next 10 minutes?

How can you make that a "step up" from the usual?

(Be it a meeting, an email, an exchange with a colleague, whatever.)

MICHAEL BUNGAY STANIER

JULY
11

Kakorraphiaphobia is a fancy word for fear of failure.

What would you do if you had no fear?

Are you portraying yourself as invincible, a rock in a stormy sea?

How easy does that make it for people to help you?

Today, face up to a truth about yourself.

MICHAEL BUNGAY STANIER

What's the perfect - truly perfect - outcome for the situation at hand?

Once you're clear on that, figure out the path back from there to where you currently stand.

Go find someone two levels up or two levels down and have a conversation with them. It will be refreshing for everyone to get out of his or her small pond.

Salt helps bring out flavour in food. And salt also has the same root as the word salary. Stick with me as I make this leap.

How might you earn your pay cheque today by "seasoning" something you're working on?

MICHAEL BUNGAY STANIER

Are you defending the status quo or are you shifting it?

(One's not necessarily better than the other. You just want to be clear where you stand.)

MICHAEL BUNGAY STANIER

Just walk away.

JULY
18

That person who's driving you crazy?

How are they a reflection of your own shadow side?

(In other words, what if it was about you rather than about them?)

MICHAEL BUNGAY STANIER

Which one is best for you today:

Stick to the shoreline?

Or head towards the open ocean?

JULY
20

What's the fun thing you can work on today? (Really. Have fun. Try it.)

MICHAEL BUNGAY STANIER

All good things come to those who wait.

Those who hesitate are lost.

Which would serve you best today?

JULY
22

WISDOM

What I Should Do On Monday.

LET'S PRETEND TODAY IS MONDAY.

A baker's dozen is 13: 12 plus a bonus for being good.

Who deserves a bonus something in your life?

Embrace what you've been resisting.

MICHAEL BUNGAY STANIER

Here's a great way to start any conversation: "How can I help?" It gets things clear, rather than you rushing off and doing what you think needs to be done (and probably doesn't).

Today let it go.

MICHAEL BUNGAY STANIER

Where can you hide so you can get some real work done today?

JULY
28

If this was a story and you were the hero… Who's the dragon? Who's got your back? Who's the evil mastermind? What's the strategy? Who are you rescuing? What's the happy ending?

The probability of getting poker's best hand
- A Royal Flush -
is 649,739 to 1.

Are you playing the cards in your hand or the cards you're wishing for?

MICHAEL BUNGAY STANIER

What are the top three projects you're working on?

How about you stop or delay or put on the back burner all that other stuff?

MICHAEL BUNGAY STANIER

What if today your default answer was No instead of Yes?

AUGUST
1

Don't judge a book by its cover.

Clothes make the man.

Which would serve you best today?

MICHAEL BUNGAY STANIER

Get to the heart of the issue. What's the real challenge here for you?

AUGUST
3

What's the easiest thing to do?

MICHAEL BUNGAY STANIER

If what you were seeing right now is a 7/10 version of you, what would a 10/10 version look like?

Any chance of seeing some glimpses of that sometime soon?

Imagine you'd just pulled The Hanged Man from the Tarot pack.

The Hanged Man

Its message is one of a willingness to adapt to change.

How could you put that into action today?

Today, make Curiosity your guide.

AUGUST
7

When did you last really stumble? Struggle? Any chance you're playing it too safe?

MICHAEL BUNGAY STANIER

You are a lovely person.

But if you were nasty, ruthless and heartless for just a moment, what would you do differently to achieve your goals?

What does that tell you?

Seeds of success often look like seeds of rebellion.

MICHAEL BUNGAY STANIER

Time for an out-of-body experience. Imagine yourself floating above yourself. Take an objective look at what's going on.

Now, what needs to change?

Marketers talk about trial and repeat. It's relatively easy to get people to try something out. It is another thing altogether to get them coming back.

Who do you need as a repeat client?

Make the call you've been putting off.

MICHAEL BUNGAY STANIER

If you're doing ANYTHING with Powerpoint, do us all a favour and cut 50% of your slides right now.

Start with any of the ones that have something in a font size of 36 or less.

MICHAEL BUNGAY STANIER

What are you holding on to?

What if you let it go?

AUGUST
15

Start something.

Explanations (and maybe apologies) can come later.

MICHAEL BUNGAY STANIER

Spend 15 minutes deleting, trashing, shredding.

Clear your plate.

Take a walk and see how that clears your head.

MICHAEL BUNGAY STANIER

What can you make lighter?

(Less heavy, less serious, less burdensome.)

AUGUST
19

WHAT ARE YOU BEING TOLD NOT TO DO FOR NO APPARENT REASON?

DON'T WALK ON THE GRASS

MICHAEL BUNGAY STANIER

Where are you letting mediocre "success" be OK?

Quite frankly, it's more damaging than failure.

AUGUST
21

Stop following the rules.

With the exception of gravity, almost all of the rules are negotiable - someone just makes them up.

MICHAEL BUNGAY STANIER

A new way of teaching kids is to let them watch a video of the classwork at home, and then do their "homework" with the teacher in class.

What might you do to reverse the expected order of doing business today?

AUGUST
23

How are you
contributing to
the curse of
unproductive
meetings?

**What's your
role and
how can you
change that?**

AUGUST
24

MICHAEL BUNGAY STANIER

You can take it personally or you can take it professionally.

Both perspectives have a use and power.

Which one would work best for you?

Work routines are like cleaning the bathroom.

Gunk builds up, and occasionally you've got to clear it out.

Give it some elbow grease!

Where will you draw the line in the sand today?

MICHAEL BUNGAY STANIER

Are you waiting for someone to give you permission?

Take it as given. Now get going.

MICHAEL BUNGAY STANIER

Flotsam: floating wreckage. Jetsam: stuff thrown off ships. What's the wreckage you need to avoid?

What can you offload to make the passage lighter?

AUGUST
29

Frame your main project as an epic quest in which you are the hero.

Now what do you see?

MICHAEL BUNGAY STANIER

I know we're not at the mythical "paper free office" yet - but I bet 80% of the paper you've got saved you're never going to look at again.

Might be time for some serious shredding.

Cancel one meeting today.

And hold the newly freed up time for thinking time.

MICHAEL BUNGAY STANIER

Pick a role model for the day: a friend, a parent, a superhero, a fictional character, whoever feels right for you.

Live up to their standards for the next 24 hours.

SEPTEMBER
2

TIME TO BUILD A BRIDGE.

FROM WHERE? TO WHERE?

MICHAEL BUNGAY STANIER

You don't get to a strong Yes unless it's based on a clear No.

Only add if you're also subtracting.

Have you been seduced by your inbox again?

You might be mistaking it for actual work.

MICHAEL BUNGAY STANIER

I bet you can name three people who, if asked, would help you out.

The next step is, yes, ask them.

Complicated: the inside of a computer.

Complex: a human being.

One needs many rules. The other, a few core principles.

MICHAEL BUNGAY STANIER

Start acting as if you were already promoted to the next level up.

Sometimes the best stuff gets done undercover.

Don't tell anyone. Just start it and see what happens.

ESPRESSO

CHAMPAGNE

Metaphorically (and maybe literally) what's the best drink for you now?

Begin again.

MICHAEL BUNGAY STANIER

That email that's been ignored by someone who matters?

Put "[resend]" in the subject line and resend it. It might not work, but it just might.

Reassess your priorities.

MICHAEL BUNGAY STANIER

Weld together a couple of unexpected things: information, experiences, people.

Add something different into the mix and see how it plays out.

Meetings expand to fill the space they are allotted.

Given them less time and see what happens.

SEPTEMBER
15

MICHAEL BUNGAY STANIER

Positive Deviants are those who are succeeding even as others struggle.

Somehow, the PD's have found a better way to do it, even with access to the same assets.

Are you one? Who else in your sphere might be one?

Feedback: What you did.

Appreciation: Who you are.

Try a little less F and a little more A.

If "be generous" was your mantra today, what would you stop hoarding and start sharing?

MICHAEL BUNGAY STANIER

As a kid I loved to read under the covers after lights out. Illicit information is always more delicious.

What can you find out that's currently embargoed?

SEPTEMBER
20

Let's assume you're playing a role in perpetuating the status quo.

So stop pointing fingers at "Them" and look at the fingers pointing back to you.

MICHAEL BUNGAY STANIER

How do you grade yourself? I give myself an A+ (although lots of my actions I rate lower than that.)

Separating out value of self vs. value of behaviour can be clarifying.

Some problems are just wicked problems - they don't have an answer that's easy or obvious.

Sit with them, be patient and see what unravels.

travel
light

What
could you
discard?

MICHAEL BUNGAY STANIER

Do you think people are with you or against you?

What's the data for that?

MICHAEL BUNGAY STANIER

Is now the time to give up?

Or is now the time to get up?

(Both are valid answers. Which one will serve you best?)

Stop putting bubble wrap around what's happening.

MICHAEL BUNGAY STANIER

Some rules are obvious, but most rules are baked into our subconscious.

Keep an eye on yourself today and see if you can figure out what rules you're following.

Climate is what you expect. Weather is what you get.

What's the weather like? What's going on around you now?

What's the climate like? What's the norm?

Are you reacting to the weather or the climate?

SEPTEMBER
29

MICHAEL BUNGAY STANIER

Get out of your head. Remember that your body is not just a handy way of transporting your brain.

SEPTEMBER
30

TODAY, MAKE

vulnerability

YOUR GUIDE.

The origin
of the word
company
is "to break
bread with."

Have lunch
with some
people
today.

"The cobra will still bite you whether you call it cobra or Mr. Cobra."
- Indian proverb

Who are you showing too much respect?

Who might bite you in this situation?

MICHAEL BUNGAY STANIER

Try:
Less Me,
More
We.
(Or vice-
versa.)

What's the big picture you're working towards? It's easy enough to forget with all the pesky details that fill your day.

Any need to recalibrate?

OCTOBER
5

MICHAEL BUNGAY STANIER

Retreat!

(Someone once said it was simply advancing in a different direction.)

OCTOBER
6

Who's the person
who triggers you
to be a less-than-
great version
of yourself?

What do they do?
And what
do you do?

**And what could
you do differently
next time?**

Think squirrel.

What supplies do you need to get in hand for the winter ahead?

MICHAEL BUNGAY STANIER

Your calendar is telling you clearly what you really think is important.
(And by "think" I mean, "do.")

How does that stand up against what you say really matters?

MICHAEL BUNGAY STANIER

You can see the funny side in this, right?

Perhaps it's time to lighten up a little and stop taking it all too seriously.

OCTOBER
10

Is this a Yes? Or is it a No?

MICHAEL BUNGAY STANIER

What are the 5 non-negotiables about how you operate?

Write them down to make them real.

Seriously, something has to change.

Maybe you are the right person to make that happen.

MICHAEL BUNGAY STANIER

A UK hi-fi store, Richer Sounds, have what they call a 'cut the crap committee' to help them keep focused on their Great Work. Is that not awesome?

Where would your CtCC get started?

OCTOBER
14

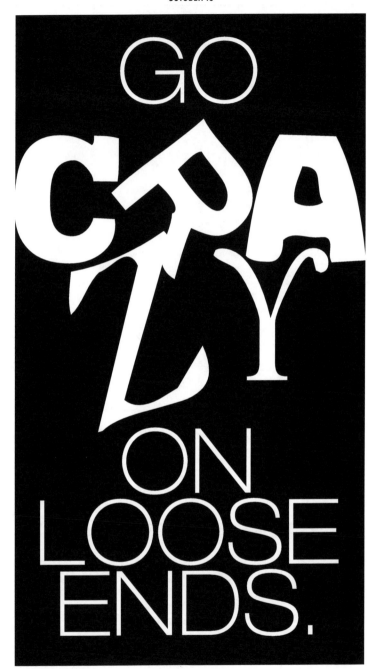

GO CRAZY ON LOOSE ENDS.

MICHAEL BUNGAY STANIER

If you had to have 10 times the impact you're having, what would have to change?

(For 10x you can't just do more of the same, faster.)

OCTOBER
16

If it's abstract, make it real.

Draw it, build it, act it.

Give the idea flesh.

MICHAEL BUNGAY STANIER

Sometimes being the expert means you've stopped hearing and seeing what's new.

What if expert = asking awesome questions?

What question would serve you well now?

You're quite possibly possibly overusing your key strength.

Take a look.

Where might you rein it in a little?

OCTOBER
19

MICHAEL BUNGAY STANIER

Ask someone, "What's on your mind?"

Get curious as to where the conversation takes you.

OCTOBER
20

Given the choice between downloading information onto someone or sparking their curiosity, I try and go for the latter.

Conversation is nearly always more useful than a monologue.

Can you move from Tell to Inquiry today?

OCTOBER

21

SIGN UP TO GET MORE GREAT WORK PROVOCATIONS AT
WWW.BOXOFCRAYONS.BIZ/PROVOKED

REMOVE A HURDLE FOR SOMEONE TODAY.

MICHAEL BUNGAY STANIER

Why not force the issue today?

Make something really happen.

MICHAEL BUNGAY STANIER

You've got short-term obligations: stuff due today, next week, next month....

But what's the bigger game you're working on?

Are those short-term goals serving that end?

Don't confuse
diagnosis
with verdict.

Where
are you
collapsing
the two
at the
moment?

OCTOBER
25

MICHAEL BUNGAY STANIER

Stop taking it all so seriously.

Really. In 10 years will you remember what you were fretting about?

In 100 years will anybody care?

This too will pass.

A team is the most powerful unit of change.

What change is your team championing?

How are you being counter-cultural?

MICHAEL BUNGAY STANIER

What might you have over-simplified?

WHO are YOU PANDERING to?

HOW'S THAT working out for YOU?

MICHAEL BUNGAY STANIER

Forget, for the moment, the pluses and minuses of the situation at hand.

Step back and ask, "What's interesting here?"

Imagine your role is to be an awesome follower.

Who is taking the lead? And how do you lift your game?

MICHAEL BUNGAY STANIER

You've been sitting on something that's been making you uncomfortable.

Perhaps now's the time to speak up.

Find someone and ask them this: What should we stop doing? What do we need to start doing? And what should we be doing a whole lot more of?

And don't let them get away with, "I don't know."

MICHAEL BUNGAY STANIER

In the gaming world they talk about leveling up.

What monsters do you have to conquer, resources collect and puzzles solve to get to the next level?

NOVEMBER
3

King Lear had
The Fool to tell
him the hard
truth of what
was really
going on.

Who's your Fool?
What's the truth
of the matter
that you're
ignoring?

WE CAN'T SEE THE DARK SIDE OF THE MOON. APPARENTLY, IT'S MUCH MORE RUGGED AND MOUNTAINOUS THAN THE SMOOTH FACE WE SEE EVERY NIGHT.

WHAT'S YOUR DARK SIDE? IF YOU SHINE A LIGHT THERE, WHAT DOES IT REVEAL?

MICHAEL BUNGAY STANIER

Are you creating autonomy or breeding dependence?

MICHAEL BUNGAY STANIER

What are you up against today?

What's your hypothesis of what's going on?

What's your data for that?

What's changed now?

What's your role in what's going on at the moment?

Knowing that, what do you need to do that's different?

MICHAEL BUNGAY STANIER

Patient.
Impatient.
They're both
useful states
of mind
(except when
they're not).
Which one do
you plan to
deploy today?

Say Thank You to someone today.

(Feel free to keep going after the first one if you'd like.)

MICHAEL BUNGAY STANIER

Micro-managing is just a subtle form of persecution.

NOVEMBER
11

SHINY OBJECT SYNDROME.

Surely I'm not the only one getting distracted by those bright baubles.

MICHAEL BUNGAY STANIER

Think of the most annoying person on your team at the moment.

How is their behavior a mirror for you?

How are they reminding you of you?

How much time do you think you spend actually thinking during the day?

Too much? Or too little?

NOVEMBER

14

MICHAEL BUNGAY STANIER

Today, make Empathy your guide.

What's the promise you've made and haven't kept?

What's the promise you've been made and it hasn't been honored?

What needs to happen now?

MICHAEL BUNGAY STANIER

If how you're doing it now is "economy class", what would the "business class" version look like?

How can you get some of that?

Can you see the gap between your mask and that more authentic self?

What if you took the mask off for a moment?

99.9999999999999% OF AN ATOM'S VOLUME IS EMPTY SPACE.

And everything we see and touch is made exclusively of atoms. What are you assuming is solid that might in fact be less than?

MICHAEL BUNGAY STANIER

They say, what gets measured gets done. Also, what gets measured gets manipulated.

In either case: what are your three key metrics for the day, for the month, for the year?

NOVEMBER
20

MICHAEL BUNGAY STANIER

Could you be "rescuing" the situation by doing some work over? Sure, there's short-term benefit. But what might be a longer-term cost? And who's going to pay?

Do you know what each member of your team's Great Work is?

Do you know what your boss's Great Work is?

Go have a conversation or ten and find out.

MICHAEL BUNGAY STANIER

What's in your trophy cabinet (metaphorical or literal)?

What is it time to discard? (Are you living on past glories?)

What's it time to add? (What's the next big challenge?)

What's your "not the typical industry news and information" reading source? (This is your inoculation against knowing more and more about less and less until you know everything about nothing.)

MICHAEL BUNGAY STANIER

To paraphrase Isaac Asimov, the most exciting thing to hear when something new is discovered in science is not "Eureka!" but "That's funny…."

What feels a little odd to you? Is it worth investigating?

THE HUMMINGBIRD. THE ELEPHANT. YOU.

ALL HAVE GOT THE SAME NUMBER OF HEARTBEATS IN A LIFE (SOMEWHERE BETWEEN A BILLION AND 1.5 BILLION).

HOW MANY DO YOU HAVE TO GO DO YOU THINK?

MICHAEL BUNGAY STANIER

Take 5 minutes at the start of the day to write down what this day is really about - and what you need to do and who you need to be to make it happen. If that felt useful, consider making it a regular routine.

Confirmation bias means you find what you're looking for, you find the evidence to prove what you want to prove and you miss other stuff.

What are you trying to prove?

What evidence are you collecting to do so?

MICHAEL BUNGAY STANIER

When Michael Jordan gave up basketball for minor league baseball, he told people failure he could live with, but he couldn't live with not trying.

What's the bold thing that might not work that you might try?

What do you wish was happening instead?

What if you had to find evidence that it already was?

MICHAEL BUNGAY STANIER

What's the lazy thing to do?

DECEMBER

1

You've probably got some sort of official title or designation at work. It's probably a little boring.
If you had a title that reflected the best of what you brought to the party, what might it be?

How about those on your team?

DRESS STRIP
IT IT
UP. BACK.

WHICH STRATEGY
WOULD SERVE
YOU BEST?

MICHAEL BUNGAY STANIER

Where today do you choose to stand on the spectrum of Conceal or Reveal?

What changes as a result?

MICHAEL BUNGAY STANIER

The Pacific Ocean is larger than all the world's landmasses put together.

What would it take to push your boat out into the unknown today?

Is your strategy a predictable one or an unconventional one?
Would it be worth considering something other than the bleeding obvious?

MICHAEL BUNGAY STANIER

Who can you give the credit to, before you take some for yourself?

It takes 8.3 minutes for light to travel from the Sun to Earth.

Give something an intense 498 seconds of your attention and see what gets illuminated.

MICHAEL BUNGAY STANIER

Who's playing mind games with you?

Even trickier, how are you playing mind games with yourself?

DECEMBER
9

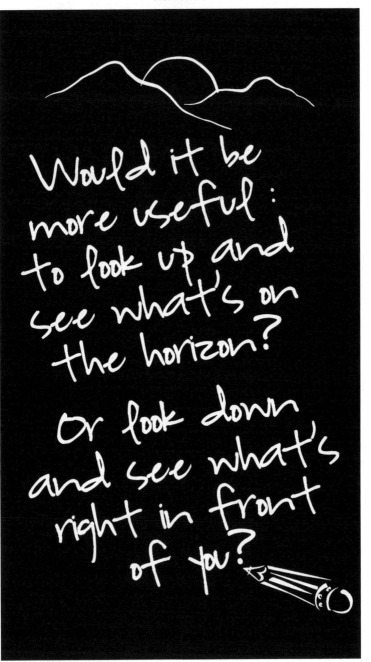

Would it be more useful: to look up and see what's on the horizon?

Or look down and see what's right in front of you?

Surprise someone today.

DECEMBER
11

Are you doing the fast and easy thing or the bigger, slower thing?

(Either one might be the best choice. Just so long as you are mindfully making that choice.)

MICHAEL BUNGAY STANIER

Anxiety is that tap on the shoulder that says, "Hey! Something important is happening here."

You're on the edge of something that matters.
Pay attention.

Are you trudging or are you bouncing?

MICHAEL BUNGAY STANIER

How might
you better
use the
wisdom
that's in
the room
with you?

Forget polishing and perfection.

Turn this into a fast prototype and go show it, test it, try it.

CUT THE BOTTOM 10%.

TASKS. PRODUCTS. PROCESSES. MEETINGS. EMAIL. YOU GET THE GIST.

MICHAEL BUNGAY STANIER

Try this question in a meeting today (even if it's with yourself):

What do you want?

MICHAEL BUNGAY STANIER

Close something down.

DECEMBER
19

How's your influence muscle? Getting a regular workout? Or turning to flab?

MICHAEL BUNGAY STANIER

What - if you're truly honest - are you valuing most here?

Success? Or your character?

DECEMBER
21

"Abandon it" is a worthwhile strategy.

MICHAEL BUNGAY STANIER

Manage up today.

DECEMBER
23

Bruce Feirstein once said, "Never settle with words what you can accomplish with a flame-thrower."

Time to stop talking and start igniting?

There's one thing to be done today that really matters. Make sure you get around to it.

DECEMBER
25

In a nice way, try being intolerant today.

Stop perpetuating mediocrity.

MICHAEL BUNGAY STANIER

The best stage direction in Shakespeare is, "Exit, pursued by a bear".

What's the bear that's chasing you?

There's an amber light for something you're working on.

Time to speed up or to brake?

MICHAEL BUNGAY STANIER

You know more than you think you do.

If you really trusted yourself, what would you do?

Start something.

Don't wait any longer for permission to do what you want to do.

DECEMBER

30

SIGN UP TO GET MORE GREAT WORK PROVOCATIONS AT
WWW.BOXOFCRAYONS.BIZ/PROVOKED

i ♡ box of crayons

Coffee art took my latte from good to cool.

What can you infuse with a little magic?

MICHAEL BUNGAY STANIER

You're finished...

But not really.

You can tell this book is designed so you can *Be Provoked In Perpetuity*.

Just as you can never stand in the same river twice, when you come back to an old provocation, you'll find new ways for it to resonate.

Beyond the book

Check our our Free Stuff page on BoxOfCrayons.biz.

From our newsletter *Outside the Lines* to *Great Work Interviews* podcasts, our *Great Work Quotes* series to our *Great Work Movies*...

Take what's useful, leave what's not.

Here's to a little more provocation in our lives.

Where Did I Get That Fact?

Jan 1 – Of course this is an estimate. The height of Mt Everest has been estimated at anywhere between 8848-8850 metres and calculating how many stories a building has depends on many factors – the Council on Tall Buildings and Urban Habitat offers three different calculators on its website.

Feb 12 – "Are We All Less Risky and More Skillful Than Our Fellow Drivers?" - Ola SVENSON, Department of Psychology, University of Stockholm, Sweden, 1981.

May 3 – part of the 4 stages of learning a new skill, attributed to Abraham Maslow, and described by Noel Burch, Gordon Training International.

May 7 - International Satellite Cloud Climatology Project (ISCCP)

May 21 – see Samuel Brannan's biography for example

June 6 – quoted in The Week, Nov 3, 2012

June 25 – see Duchenne Smile and FACS (Facial Action Coding System)

July 5 – The Power of Habit: Why We Do What We Do in Life and Business , Charles Duhigg

July 30 – About.com Statistics

August 23 – Flip Teaching

September 16 – PositiveDeviance.org

October 14 – The Richer Way, Julian Richer

November 26 – Heartbeat Hypothesis, Wikipedia

December 24 – BrainyQuote.com

Acknowledgments

Thanks are due to our brilliant designer Ana Garza-Robilliard, who brings life to my words here and in blazing colour weekly on the Great Work Blog. This is our third book together, all of them as elegant and beautiful as you Ana.

Thank you VP of Everything Else at Box of Crayons for keeping all the plates spinning while also doing the editing and proofreading.

Thanks also to our Publishing Navigator, Janica Smith for helping us get this little book out to the world.

Thanks are due to every Great Work Provocations subscriber who took the time to tell us the ways in which these little messages challenged, comforted, annoyed, amazed, prodded or poked them. Thank you. We love hearing from you.

Made in the USA
Charleston, SC
30 March 2015